First edition for the United States and Canada published 1994 by
Barron's Educational Series, Inc.

English translation © Copyright 1994 by Greta Kilburn.

© Copyright 1993 Uitgeverij Zwijsen Algemeen B.V.
Tilburg/Dinie Akkerman (text and illustrations)

Originally published in the Netherlands by Elzenga, Tilburg
The title of the Dutch edition is *Koning zijn, is dat fijn?*
Translated from the Dutch by Greta Kilburn.

All inquiries should be addressed to:
Barron's Educational Series, Inc.
250 Wireless Boulevard
Hauppauge, NY 11788

International Standard Book No. 0-8120-6430-5 (hardcover)
0-8120-1957-1 (paperback)
Library of Congress Catalog Card No. 93-50940

Library of Congress Cataloging-in-Publication Data

Akkerman, Dinie.
    [Koning zijn, is dat fijn? English]
    King on the beach / pictures and text by Dinie Akkerman :
translated from the Dutch by Greta Kilburn.
       p. cm.
    "Originally published in the Netherlands by Elzenga, Tilburg
[under the title] Koning zijn, is dat fijn?" — T.p. verso.
    Summary: When Oscar the Elephant is crowned king, he builds
himself such a high throne that he can no longer see his friends.
    ISBN 0-8120-6430-5 (hardcover). — ISBN 0-8120-1957-1 (pbk.)
    [1. Kings, queens, rulers, etc —Fiction. 2. Elephants—Fiction.
3. Animals—Fiction. 4. Friendship—Fiction.] I. Kilburn, Greta.
II. Title.
PZ7.A312Ki   1994
[E]—dc20

          93-50940
          CIP
          AC

PRINTED IN BELGIUM
4567   4900   987654321

King on the Beach

Pictures and Text by Dinie Akkerman
Translated from the Dutch by Greta Kilburn

BARRON'S

Oscar the elephant was taking a nap in the sun.

"Let him sleep," said Sara.

"We'll make a garland for him."

Paco helped by picking the flowers.

Sara strung them together.

"Look, Oscar," said Sara.

"We made a crown for you.

You're a king now."

Oscar the elephant felt very happy.

"I think being a king," he beamed, "would be so much fun."

Oscar proudly looked around.

"I really should have a throne.

A very tall one so I can see my entire country."

He walked off and came back with a hammer, wood, and nails.

"I'm going to make a throne out of my chair," he told Sara and Paco.

He built three steps on each side of his chair.

"Let's see how this feels."

Oscar climbed up on his throne.

"This isn't quite right yet," he said.

"There's still too much country I can't see."

Oscar went back to work.

The chair got taller and taller.

Everyone came to watch King Oscar work on his throne.

Oscar built until there were twenty-five steps on each side of his chair.
By that time he was satisfied that it was high enough.
King Oscar climbed up to his throne.
He climbed and climbed and climbed . . . .

When he finally reached the top,
he could look all around across the whole country and the ocean.
Cobus Crow landed on the arm of his throne.
"A big cookie," he said, "from your friends down below."
"Being a King," said Oscar, "is very nice,
especially with such wonderful friends.
Too bad they're so far away."

Suddenly it started to rain.
Not gently, but very, very hard.
Soaking wet, Oscar climbed down.
He climbed and climbed and climbed . . . .

Down below Oscar said,
"Achoo, achoooo, achoooooooo!!!"
Then he said, "I didn't know that kings
could get colds like this."

"Off to bed," said Doctor Rabbit.
"It is much too cold on that throne.
Now, three times a day take three drops of this medicine
dissolved in water or lemonade or . . ."
"Lemonade is fine," said Oscar before he fell fast asleep.

"If he goes back to that cold throne," said Sara,

"his cold will come back in no time at all."

Doctor Rabbit pulled his hat a little further down over his eyes.

This way he could not see anything at all, but he could think much better.

"The best thing to do" said Doctor Rabbit after a while,

"is to raise the whole house. Then the throne can just stay inside

so that Oscar won't have to sit outside."

While Oscar was asleep,
his friends rushed back and forth with hammers,
nails, and lots and lots of poles.

They worked all day until it started
to get dark.
By then the house was just
as high as Oscar's throne.

Then they put
the throne inside.

When Oscar woke up in the morning,
his house was standing
on a whole lot of poles.
He sat down on his throne
by the window.
"Just as always," he thought,
"except much higher."
Oscar looked out the window.
He could see the whole country
and he could see the ocean.
But he could not see his friends.
They were so far away, all the way down . . . .

Down below were Sara and Paco
and all Oscar's friends.
They looked up and missed him.
"Does he really have to be a king?"
they wondered.
"Do kings always have to sit so high?"

"We might be able to make a small mountain,"
Sara said softly, "To be closer to him . . . ."
"A big mountain would help more, of course," said Doctor Rabbit.
Then they all started to rush around with pails and shovels.
They dug and they shoveled and they carried sand.
They worked all day long.

The mountain grew and grew.

That night, when all the stars were
twinkling in the sky, the mountain
was finally high enough.
They knocked on Oscar's door.
"Visitors," cried Oscar.
"Come in, come in!
I missed you all so much!"

Then they drank lemonade and ate cookies
in Oscar's house on the mountain.
They looked through the window and admired the view.
"You have so many stars, Oscar!"
"Yes," said Oscar, "I have a wonderful place here.
A little bit higher than before so that you can tell
I was a king for a while."